# GOD IS CLOSE
# TO
# THE BROKENHEARTED

**MELANIE MARTIN**

# TABLE OF CONTENTS

# ACKNOWLEDGMENTS

Writing this book was a journey of healing and hope for me, and I could not have done it without the support and encouragement of many people.

First and foremost, I want to thank God, who is the source of my strength, my peace, and my joy. He is the one who healed my broken heart and gave me a new purpose and a new vision. He is the one who inspired me to write this book and share my story with others. To Him be all the glory and honor.

I also want to thank my family, Antonio, Asia'anna and Destiny who stood by me through the darkest and most difficult times of my life. They were always there to comfort me, to listen to me, and to pray for me. They were always there to remind me of God's love and faithfulness. They were always there to celebrate with me every milestone and every victory. I am so blessed and grateful to have them in my life.

I also want to thank my friends, who were like angels sent by God to help me along the way. They were always there to offer me their friendship, their wisdom, and their kindness. They were always there to cheer me up, to lift me up, and to inspire me. They were always there to challenge me, to motivate me, and to empower me. I am so thankful and appreciative of their presence in my life.

Last but not least, I want to thank you, the reader, who is the reason why I wrote this book. You are the one who gave me the opportunity, the privilege, and the joy of sharing my story with you. You are the one who gave me the feedback, the appreciation, and the encouragement that kept me going. You are the one who gave me the hope, the inspiration, and the purpose that made this book possible. I am so humbled and touched by your interest and your support.

Thank you all for being a part of my journey and for making this book a reality. I hope that this book will bless you, inspire you, and empower you to overcome your heartbreak and to discover the amazing plans that God has for you.

# INTRODUCTION

## *Why I Wrote This Book*

Have you ever experienced heartbreak? Have you ever felt the pain of losing someone or something that you love? Have you ever wondered how to cope with the emotions that overwhelm you? Have you ever questioned God's presence and purpose in your life?

If you answered yes to any of these questions, then this book is for you.

I wrote this book because I know what it is like to go through heartbreak. I know what it is like to feel the agony of separation, the anger of betrayal, the fear of loneliness, the guilt of regret, and the despair of hopelessness. I know what it is like to cry out to God and ask Him why He allowed this to happen, and what He wants me to do.

I wrote this book because I also know what it is like to find healing and hope in God. I know what it is like to experience His comfort, His peace, His grace, and His joy. I know what it is like to discover His love, His faithfulness, His plan, and His purpose. I know what it is like to trust Him and follow Him, and to see Him work miracles in my life.

I wrote this book because I want to share my story with you. I want to share with you how I went from being brokenhearted to being wholehearted. I want to share with you how I learned to rely on God, to pray to Him, and to listen to Him. I want to share with you how I found strength, courage, and wisdom in His word, His promises, and His character. I want to share with you how I grew, changed, and transformed through His power, His presence, and His spirit.

I wrote this book because I want to help you with your own heartbreak. I want to help you understand what it means to be brokenhearted, and how you can overcome it. I want to help you cope with the different stages of grief, and how they relate to your heartbreak. I want to help you find the benefits of having a community and support, and how they can help you heal. I want to help you explore the road to forgiveness, and how they can free you from bitterness. I want to help you embrace the art of self-discovery and growth, and how they can enrich your life. I want to help you cultivate the power of gratitude and joy, and how they can transform your perspective.

I wrote this book because I want to inspire you, comfort you, and empower you. I want to inspire you to believe that God is close to the brokenhearted and that He can heal your wounds and restore your joy. I want to comfort you with the assurance that you are not alone, that you are not hopeless, and that you are not broken beyond repair. I want to empower you to live with a grateful and joyful heart, and to look forward to a new beginning and a brighter future.

This book is not a magic formula or a quick fix. It is not a set of rules or but a list of steps to guide you to your healing. It is not a lecture or a sermon. It is a conversation, a testimony, and a journey. It is a conversation between you and me and between you and God. It is a testimony of God's goodness, grace, and glory in my life. It is a journey of healing, hope, and happiness that I invite you to join me on.

I hope that this book will bless you, touch you, and change you. I hope that this book will be a friend, a guide, and a companion to you. I hope that this book will be a gift, a treasure, and a blessing to you.

Thank you for choosing this book. Thank you for reading this book. Thank you for being a part of this book.

### *Prayer from September 22, 2023*

*I really don't know what to write anymore. I feel down right now! I don't know what to pray! I don't want to feel this way at all. I feel like my life is passing me by and I'm always in survival mode. I want to relax, I want peace, I don't want to worry or stress. I want good health. I need to hear from God. I want to take care of my family. Another day has passed. Another 24 hours went by and we are still in the same situation. We need a sudden blessing. A sudden breakthrough and change. Haven't we been through enough? I've always tried to do what I thought was right but for some reason, I always get let down or done wrong. Where is my Job or Joseph's moment? Where I get back triple for my trouble. Where I go from the bottom to the top. I can't keep listening to these motivational videos saying the same thing over and over again, especially when I don't see anything happening. I need to see you move God in our situation. I feel like I made a mistake and am now being punished for it. Where is our miracle, sign, and wonder? Where is our home? Where is our peace? Why do we have to wait so long? We have already been through so much pain! Father, do You hear me? Are You listening? We need to see our blessings here on earth. We need You to show us our promises here on earth. Guide my mind and heart. I don't want to be like this or feel this way. I don't want to hurt anymore. I don't want to be embarrassed or humiliated again. Father, I'm heartbroken. Nothing seems to be going right for us. No home, no job, no money, no savings, no plan, and no idea what we are doing. Help us, help me I just want to do your will, Father. What's my purpose here? What do I need to know? What do I need to do? Your plans are bigger than my plans. Your ways are bigger than my ways. You know the plans You have for us. Guide me, lead me. Turn this situation in our favor. Show us you, Father. You're bigger than anything we're going through. There is no way I should ever feel this low when you God, are my Father. Just like my natural father when I ask for something I get it. So I know You being the creator of this world will give me more than I can think or ask. Please don't let another day go by without your hand touching our life and performing a miracle in our situation. Please Father help us!*

*Love your daughter, Melanie*

### *Prayer from October 25, 2023*

*Dear Heavenly Father, we have been without a home for 22 days. We have been without a home of our own for three months, two weeks, and four days. I know you know, but I feel defeated. I feel hopeless. I feel unworthy. I feel lost. I feel like I failed my family. I feel sad. I feel angry. I feel stupid. I feel embarrassed. I feel upset. I feel like things aren't changing. What can I do Lord to help me cope with the situation? Help me, father! I need your help now! Please step in and change this for us. Please help us! I have no more fight left in me! I need your help!*

*Your daughter, Melanie*

# CHAPTER 1

## *What Does It Mean To Be Brokenhearted?*

To be brokenhearted is to experience a deep and overwhelming sense of sadness, loss, and grief. It is to feel as if your heart has been shattered into pieces, and you don't know how to put them back together. It is to suffer from emotional pain that affects your whole being, your thoughts, your feelings, and your actions.

Being brokenhearted can happen for many reasons. It can be caused by the end of a romantic relationship, the death of a loved one, the betrayal of a friend, the failure of a dream, or any other situation that makes you feel rejected, abandoned, or alone. Being brokenhearted can also happen for no apparent reason, as a result of depression, anxiety, or other mental health issues.

Being brokenhearted is not a sign of weakness, nor is it something to be ashamed of. It is a natural and normal human response to loss and trauma. It is a way of coping with the changes and challenges that life brings. It is a part of the healing process that allows you to grow and learn from your experiences.

Being brokenhearted is not a permanent state, nor is it a hopeless one. It is a temporary and transitional phase that will eventually pass, as you find ways to heal and move on. It is a journey that will take time, patience, and courage, but also one that will bring you new opportunities, insights, and strengths.

Being brokenhearted is not a solitary experience, nor is it one that you have to face alone. It is a common and shared experience that connects you with others who have gone through similar situations. It is an opportunity to seek and receive support, comfort, and guidance from those who care about you. It is a chance to build and strengthen your relationships with yourself, with others, and with God.

In this chapter, we will explore what it means to be heartbroken, and how you can cope with it in healthy and positive ways. We will look at the causes, symptoms, and different ways heartbreak manifest.

Heartbreak is a universal human experience that can affect anyone, regardless of age, gender, culture, or background. It is the emotional pain that we feel when we lose someone or something that we love, value, or care about deeply.

## Heartbreak can be caused by various situations, such as:

❖ The end of a romantic relationship, either by breakup, divorce, or death.

❖ The loss of a friendship, either by betrayal, conflict, or distance.

❖ The death of a loved one, such as a family member, a pet, or a close friend.

❖ The disappointment of unfulfilled expectations, dreams, or goals.

❖ The rejection of someone we admire, respect, or desire.

❖ The failure of something we worked hard for, such as a career, a project, or a test.

## Heartbreak can manifest in different ways, such as:

❖ Sadness, sorrow, or grief.

❖ Anger, resentment, or bitterness.

❖ Fear, anxiety, or insecurity.

❖    Guilt, shame, or regret.

❖    Loneliness, isolation, or withdrawal.

❖    Confusion, doubt, or uncertainty.

❖    Numbness, emptiness, or apathy.

## Heartbreak can affect different aspects of our lives, such as:

❖    Our physical health, by causing symptoms such as insomnia, fatigue, headaches, chest pain, or loss of appetite.

❖    Our mental health, by causing conditions such as depression, anxiety, post-traumatic stress disorder, or suicidal thoughts.

❖    Our emotional health, by affecting our mood, self-esteem, motivation, or happiness.

❖    Our social health, by impacting our relationships, communication, or trust with others.

❖    Our spiritual health, by challenging our faith, beliefs, or values.

Heartbreak is not a sign of weakness, but a sign of strength. It shows that we have the capacity to love, to care, and to feel deeply. It also shows that we have the potential to heal, to grow, and to overcome.

In this book, I will share with you my personal story of how I experienced heartbreak, and how I found healing and hope through faith, prayer, and God's grace. I will also share with you some practical tips and insights that can help you cope with your own heartbreak, and guide you towards a path of recovery and renewal.

I hope that this book will inspire you, comfort you, and empower you to face your heartbreak with courage and confidence. I hope that this book will remind you that you are not alone, that you are not hopeless, and that you are not broken beyond repair. I hope that this book will help you discover that God is close to the brokenhearted and that He can heal your wounds and restore your joy.

# CHAPTER 2

## *The Importance Of Faith: How Faith Can Help Us Through Difficult Times*

Life is full of challenges and hardships. Sometimes, we may feel overwhelmed by the problems we face, such as illness, loss, conflict, or stress. We may wonder why God allows us to suffer, or if He even cares about us. We may feel hopeless, angry, or depressed.

I know for me when my husband was shot and became paralyzed from the waist down I felt overwhelmed and wondered how could God do this to us. What was the lesson in me having to take care of two infants and a man who was used to taking care of himself. I wasn't strong enough for this and I had no support. I felt alone.

But in difficult times like these, we can find strength and comfort in our faith. Faith is not just a belief in God, but a trust in His love, power, and plan for us. Faith is not a denial of reality, but a recognition of God's presence and purpose in it. Faith is not a passive acceptance, but an active cooperation with God's will.

## Here are some ways that faith can help us through difficult times:

❖ **Faith reminds us that God is with us:** God has promised never to leave us or forsake us (Hebrews 13:5). He is always watching over us, listening to us, and working for us. He knows what we are going through, and He cares about us. He is our refuge and strength, an ever-present help in trouble (Psalm 46:1). He is the source of our peace, joy, and hope. When we feel alone or afraid, we can turn to Him in prayer and praise, and experience His presence and comfort.

❖ **Faith helps us to see God's perspective:** God's ways are higher than our ways, and His thoughts are higher than our thoughts (Isaiah 55:8-9). He has a plan and a purpose for everything that happens, even if we don't understand it or like it. He can use our difficulties to shape us, teach us, and bless us. He can also use them to glorify Himself and to advance His kingdom. When we trust in His wisdom and sovereignty, we can have peace and confidence in His outcomes.

❖ **Faith enables us to grow in character and maturity:** God uses difficult times to test and refine our faith like gold is refined by fire (1 Peter 1:6-7). He wants us to become more like Christ, who endured suffering and temptation, yet remained faithful and obedient to God (Hebrews 12:1-3). He wants us to develop the fruits of the Spirit, such as love, joy, peace, patience, kindness, goodness, faithfulness, gentleness, and self-control (Galatians 5:22-23). When we rely on His grace and power, we can overcome our weaknesses and sins, and become stronger and holier.

❖ **Faith inspires us to serve others and share the gospel:** God does not want us to waste our pain, but to use it for His glory and for the good of others. He wants us to comfort others with the comfort we have received from Him (2 Corinthians 1:3-4). He wants us to be a light and a salt in the world, showing His love and truth to those who are hurting and lost (Matthew 5:13-16). He wants us to proclaim the gospel of His salvation, and to make disciples of all nations (Matthew 28:18-20). When we follow His example and

His command, we can find meaning and joy in our suffering, and make a positive impact in the world.

Faith is not a magic wand that makes our problems disappear, but a lifeline that connects us to God, who is the solution to our problems. Faith is not a guarantee that we will not face difficulties, but an assurance that we will not face them alone, or in vain. Faith is not wishful thinking, but a confident expectation that God will fulfill His promises, and accomplish His purposes.

Therefore, let us hold on to our faith, and let it help us through difficult times. Let us remember that God is with us, that He has a plan for us, and that He is working for us. Let us trust in His love, power, and wisdom, and cooperate with His will. Let us grow in His grace, and reflect His glory. Let us serve His people, and share His gospel.

### *Revelation 21:4*

*And let us look forward to the day when He will wipe away every tear from our eyes, and there will be no more death, mourning, crying, or pain, for the old order of things will have passed away.*

# CHAPTER 3

## *The Role Of Prayer: The Importance Of Prayer In The Healing Process*

Prayer is a powerful tool that God has given us to communicate with Him, express our emotions, seek His guidance, and receive His healing. Prayer is especially important when we are going through the pain of a broken heart, whether it is caused by a breakup, a divorce, a death, a betrayal, or any other loss.

When we are brokenhearted, we may feel a range of emotions, such as sadness, anger, guilt, fear, or loneliness. We may also experience physical symptoms, such as insomnia, fatigue, loss of appetite, or headaches. We may feel like we have lost our sense of purpose, our hope, or our faith.

But God does not want us to stay in this state of despair. He wants us to come to Him with our broken hearts, and to trust Him to heal them. He is the God who heals the brokenhearted and binds up their wounds (Psalm 147:3). He is the God who is close to the brokenhearted and saves those who are crushed in spirit (Psalm 34:18). He is the God who comforts us in all our troubles so that we can comfort those in any trouble with the comfort we ourselves receive from God (2 Corinthians 1:3-4).

## Here are some ways that prayer can help us in the healing process of being brokenhearted:

❖ **Prayer helps us to release our emotions to God:** Sometimes, we may try to suppress or deny our feelings, thinking that they are wrong or weak. But God wants us to be honest and open with Him, and to pour out our hearts before Him (Psalm 62:8). He can handle our emotions, and He understands what we are going through. He is not offended by our anger, nor ashamed of our tears. He is compassionate and gracious, slow to anger and abounding in love (Psalm 103:8). When we express our emotions to God, we allow Him to heal them, and to fill us with His peace and joy.

❖ **Prayer helps us to receive God's perspective on our situation:** Sometimes, we may have a distorted or limited view of our situation, focusing only on the negative aspects, or blaming ourselves or others for what happened. But God sees the bigger picture, and He knows the plans He has for us, plans to prosper us and not to harm us, plans to give us hope and a future (Jeremiah 29:11). He can use our pain for a greater purpose, to shape us, to teach us, and to bless us. He can also use it to glorify Himself and to advance His kingdom. When we seek God's perspective on our situation, we can have faith and confidence in His outcomes.

❖ **Prayer helps us to receive God's grace and strength to cope with our situation:** Sometimes, we may feel overwhelmed or helpless by our situation, thinking that we cannot handle it, or that we have no resources to deal with it. But God is our refuge and strength, an ever-present help in trouble (Psalm 46:1). He is able to do immeasurably more than all we ask or imagine, according to His power that is at work within us (Ephesians 3:20). He gives us His grace, which is sufficient for us, and His power, which is made perfect in our weakness (2 Corinthians 12:9). When we rely on

God's grace and strength, we can overcome our challenges, and become more resilient and courageous.

❖ **Prayer helps us to restore our relationship with God and others:** Sometimes, we may feel distant or estranged from God or others, thinking that they have abandoned us, or that they do not care about us. But God is faithful, and He will never leave us nor forsake us (Hebrews 13:5). He loves us with everlasting love, and He has engraved us on the palms of His hands (Jeremiah 31:3; Isaiah 49:16). He also calls us to love one another, as He has loved us (John 13:34). He wants us to forgive those who have hurt us, as He has forgiven us (Colossians 3:13). He wants us to reconcile with those who have offended us, as He has reconciled us to Himself (2 Corinthians 5:18). When we restore our relationship with God and others, we can experience His healing, and His peace that transcends all understanding (Philippians 4:7).

Prayer is not a magic formula that makes our problems disappear, but a vital connection that links us to God, who is the solution to our problems. Prayer is not a guarantee that we will not face difficulties, but an assurance that we will not face them alone, or in vain. Prayer is not wishful thinking, but a confident expectation that God will fulfill His promises, and accomplish His purposes.

Therefore, let us pray without ceasing (1 Thessalonians 5:17), and let it help us in the healing process of being brokenhearted. Let us remember that God is with us, that He has a plan for us, and that He is working for us. Let us receive His love, His perspective, His grace, and His strength. Let us restore our relationship with Him and others. And let us look forward to the day when He will wipe away every tear from our eyes, and there will be no more death, mourning, crying, or pain.

# CHAPTER 4

## *The Nature Of God: How God Heals Our Wounds And Restores Our Joy*

We all have wounds in our lives. Some are visible, some are hidden. Some are caused by others, some are self-inflicted. Some are fresh, some are old. Some are healed, some are still bleeding. Whatever the source, nature, or extent of our wounds, they affect us deeply. They cause us pain, anger, fear, shame, guilt, or sadness. They make us feel broken, unworthy, or hopeless.

Yet, God does not intend for us to dwell in our wounds; He desires us to reside in His love, to experience healing, restoration, and to revel in His peace and joy. He envisions us as whole, not broken.

God heals our wounds and restores our joy through three transformative avenues: **His grace, His truth, and His presence.**

## By His Grace

Grace is God's unmerited favor. It is His gift of love, mercy, and forgiveness. It is His power to heal, transform, and save. Grace is not something we earn, deserve, or demand. Grace is something we receive, accept, and respond to.

God's grace is the source of our healing and restoration. Without His grace, we would be stuck in our wounds, unable to heal or change. Without His grace, we would be separated from Him, unable to receive His love or forgiveness. Without His grace, we would be lost, unable to find our way or purpose.

But God, in His grace, has reached out to us. He has sent His Son, Jesus Christ, to die for our sins and to rise again, defeating death and evil. He has offered us a new life, a new identity, and a new relationship with Him. He has invited us to become His children, His friends, and His partners. He has forgiven us, accepted us, and loved us unconditionally.

All we need to do is to accept His grace, to believe in His Son, and to receive His Spirit. When we do that, we are healed from the inside out. We are freed from the guilt and shame of our sins. We are cleansed from the stains and scars of our wounds. We are filled with the love and joy of His Spirit. We are transformed into His likeness and image.

## By His Truth

Truth is God's reality. It is His word, His wisdom, and His will. It is His revelation, His instruction, and His direction. Truth is not something we create, manipulate, or ignore. Truth is something we discover, learn, and obey.

God's truth is the guide of our healing and restoration. Without His truth, we would be deceived by our wounds, unable to see or understand them. Without His truth, we would be misled by the world, unable to discern or resist it. Without His truth, we would be confused by ourselves, unable to know or grow in Him.

But God, in His truth, has spoken to us. He has given us His word, the Bible, to reveal His character, His plan, and His promises. He has given us His wisdom, the Holy Spirit, to teach us His truth, to remind us of His word, and to guide us into His will. He has given us His direction, His commands, His principles, and His examples, to show us how to live, how to love, and how to serve.

All we need to do is to embrace His truth, read His word, and listen to His Spirit. When we do that, we are enlightened from the outside in. We are exposed to the light of His truth, which reveals our wounds and their causes. We are confronted by the truth of His word, which challenges our beliefs and our vows. We are corrected by the truth of His Spirit, which convicts us of our sins and our errors.

## By His Presence

Presence is God's intimacy. It is His nearness, His involvement, and His comfort. It is His fellowship, His friendship, and His support. Presence is not something we earn, deserve, or demand. Presence is something we enjoy, appreciate, and share.

God's presence is the goal of our healing and restoration. Without His presence, we would be lonely in our wounds, unable to find or feel Him. Without His presence, we would be isolated from others, unable to connect or relate with them. Without His presence, we would be empty in ourselves, unable to satisfy or fulfill our deepest needs.

But God, in His presence, has come to us. He has become one of us, in the person of Jesus Christ, to share our humanity, our pain, and our death. He has risen from the dead, to give us His life, His power, and His glory. He has sent His Spirit, to dwell in us, to fill us, and to empower us. He has promised to never leave us, to never forsake us, and to never stop loving us.

All we need to do is to seek His presence, to pray to Him, and to worship Him. When we do that, we are connected from the inside out. We are drawn to the presence of His love, which heals our wounds and restores our joy. We are invited to the presence of His people, who support us, encourage us, and pray for us. We are welcomed to the presence of His kingdom, where we serve Him, honor Him, and glorify Him.

In conclusion, God heals our wounds and restores our joy by His grace, by His truth, and by His presence. He does it because He loves us because He cares for us, and because He wants us to be whole. He does it not only for our sake, but also for His sake, and the sake of others. He does it to display His glory, to demonstrate His power, and to declare His goodness.

Let us, therefore, receive His healing and restoration with gratitude and faith. Let us cooperate with His work in us, by surrendering to His grace, submitting to His truth, and seeking His presence. Let us celebrate His healing and restoration with joy and praise. Let us share His healing and restoration with others, by testifying of His grace, by teaching His truth, and by inviting them to His presence.

# CHAPTER 5

## The Stages Of Grief: Exploring The Different Stages Of Grief And How They Relate To Heartbreak

Heartbreak is a form of loss that can trigger a grieving process. When we lose someone we love, whether it is due to a breakup, a divorce, a death, or any other reason, we may experience a range of emotions and reactions that can be overwhelming and confusing. These emotions and reactions are not random or abnormal, but part of a natural and healthy process of coping with loss.

In early years one of the most popular and widely used models was identified in five stages of grief that people may go through after a loss: denial, anger, bargaining, depression, and acceptance. Later, two more stages were added by other researchers: shock and guilt. These seven stages are not fixed or sequential, but rather fluid and overlapping. They can vary in intensity, duration, and order for different people and different situations.

## Here are the seven stages of grief and how they relate to heartbreak:

1. **SHOCK:** This is the initial reaction to the loss, where we may feel numb, stunned, or disoriented. We may have difficulty accepting or comprehending what happened, and we may feel detached from reality. This stage serves as a protective mechanism that helps us cope with the sudden and overwhelming change in our lives.

2. **DENIAL:** This is the stage where we refuse to acknowledge or accept the reality of the loss. We may try to pretend that nothing has changed, or that the person we lost is still with us. We may avoid talking about the loss, or act as if everything is normal. This stage helps us to buffer the shock and pain of the loss, and to gradually adjust to the new situation.

3. **ANGER:** This is the stage where we express our frustration, resentment, or rage towards the person we lost, ourselves, or others. We may blame the person we lost for leaving us, or ourselves for not doing enough to prevent the loss, or others for causing or contributing to the loss. We may also feel angry at God, fate, or life for being unfair or

cruel. This stage helps us to release our pent-up emotions, and to assert our sense of control and justice.

4. **BARGAINING:** This is the stage where we try to negotiate or compromise with ourselves, the person we lost, or God, to reverse or postpone the loss. We may make promises, vows, or deals, such as "If you come back, I will do anything you want", or "If I do this, will you spare me from this pain?" This stage helps us to cope with our feelings of helplessness and hopelessness, and to seek a sense of meaning and purpose.

I remember when I was 21 years old my youngest daughter dad was in a bad car accident to the point he was unrecognizable. I didn't know what to do. My emotions were all over the place because I was pregnant with our daughter. All I knew to do at the time was to pray to God. After leaving his hospital room I tried to relax. I stood there in the family room staring at the clock, in shock. I didn't see anything changing and the doctors weren't helpful. I prayed to God and said God let him live please, I don't care if he's in a wheelchair, I promise I'll take care of him. After saying that prayer I sat down and in a dream God showed me my child's dad was leaving the hospital. I woke up and he was gone, he died. I unknowingly made a vow to God. I was bargaining with God not knowing it will change my life later on.

5. **GUILT:** This is the stage where we feel remorse, regret, or responsibility for the loss. We may think of all the things we could have done or said differently or all the things we left unsaid or undone. We may also feel guilty for surviving the loss, or for feeling any positive emotions after the loss. This stage helps us to confront our mistakes and shortcomings, and to seek forgiveness and reconciliation.

6. **DEPRESSION:** This is the stage where we feel the full impact of the loss and the emptiness and loneliness that it leaves behind. We may experience sadness, despair, hopelessness, or apathy. We may lose interest or pleasure in the things we used to enjoy, or withdraw from the people we used to connect with. We may also have physical symptoms, such as insomnia, fatigue, loss of appetite, or headaches. This stage helps us to mourn the loss, and to acknowledge and process our grief.

7. **ACCEPTANCE:** This is the stage where we come to terms with the reality and finality of the loss, and the changes that it brings to our lives. We may not feel happy or relieved, but we may feel more calm, peaceful, or hopeful. We may start to adapt to the new situation, and to

rebuild our lives without the person we lost. We may also find new ways to honor and remember the person we lost, and to cherish the memories and lessons that they left us with.

These stages of grief are not a linear or predictable progression, but a dynamic and individual process. We may experience some stages more than others, or skip some stages altogether. We may also revisit some stages at different times, or experience more than one stage at the same time. There is no right or wrong way to grieve, and no set time frame for how long it takes. The important thing is to allow ourselves to feel and express our emotions, and to seek support and guidance from others who can help us heal and grow.

# CHAPTER 6

## The Strength In Community: Navigating Brokenness With Support

Enduring heartbreak, a profoundly painful and universally human experience, has the power to leave us shattered in various dimensions of our lives. Whether prompted by a breakup, divorce, loss, or death, its impact extends beyond emotional turmoil, reaching into our sense of self, hope, and faith. Physical and mental health may suffer, resulting in insomnia, fatigue, loss of appetite, anxiety, depression, or even thoughts of suicide.

However, the journey through heartbreak need not be solitary and hopeless. The importance of having a community and support during these times becomes a crucial element in the healing process, offering a myriad of benefits:

- ❖ **Combating Isolation:** Community and support dismantle the walls of loneliness and isolation that often accompany heartbreak. Understanding that others empathize and care creates a safe space to share emotions, vent frustrations, and recount personal stories.

- ❖ **Gaining Perspective:** Amid heartbreak, distorted views of ourselves, situations, and the future can prevail. Community and support provide a clear, objective lens to challenge irrational thoughts, recognize strengths, and find purpose in pain. They aid in setting realistic expectations, coping with uncertainty, and planning for the future.

- ❖ **Facilitating Healing and Growth:** Feeling stuck and unable to move forward is a common hurdle in heartbreak. Community and support guide the healing process, fostering forgiveness, letting go of the past, and embracing the present. They open avenues to self-discovery, new interests, opportunities, and the building of fresh relationships.

**Creating a supportive community during heartbreak involves various approaches:**

❖ **Joining Support Groups:** Whether online or offline, support groups for similar situations offer a sense of belonging, empathy, and practical advice.

❖ **Leveraging Existing Networks:** Engaging with family, friends, colleagues, or neighbors provides emotional, social, and material support from those who already know and care for us.

❖ **Seeking Professional Help:** Therapists, counselors, coaches, or mentors possess the skills to guide us through heartbreak, addressing underlying issues affecting recovery.

❖ **Connecting with Identity-based Communities:** Finding people who share our identity, values, beliefs, or interests fosters acceptance, understanding, and exploration of our identity.

❖ **Volunteering:** Contributing to a cause we're passionate about not only provides fulfillment but also connects us with like-minded individuals.

Embracing community and support in times of brokenness is a testament to strength and courage, not weakness. It's a conscious effort to face and embrace the pain, honoring and remembering lost loved ones rather than forgetting or replacing them.

With a supportive community, healing becomes a more robust, transformative process, enabling us to learn, grow, and thrive in the aftermath of heartbreak, discovering new hope, joy, and love in our lives.

# CHAPTER 7

## *The Journey Of Forgiveness: Embracing Healing And Happiness*

Navigating the challenging yet rewarding path of healing from heartbreak brings us face to face with the transformative power of forgiveness. More than a singular event, forgiveness is a gradual process demanding time, patience, and courage. It doesn't entail forgetting or condoning the actions that caused pain but centers around releasing resentment and bitterness, clearing the way for healing and happiness.

The impact of forgiveness extends beyond emotional and mental well-being, reaching into the realms of physical and spiritual health. Research indicates that forgiveness can lower blood pressure, reduce stress, enhance the immune system, and boost self-esteem. Moreover, forgiveness fosters a closer connection with God, aligning us with His will and grace. As Ephesians 4:32 reminds us, "Be kind and compassionate to one another, forgiving each other, just as in Christ God forgave you."

But how can we forgive someone who has broken our heart? How do we overcome anger, pain, and betrayal to embrace a future filled with hope and trust? **Consider these steps on your journey to forgiveness:**

❖ **Acknowledge Your Feelings:** The initial step towards forgiveness involves recognizing and validating your emotions. Whether it's hurt, anger, sadness, or any other feeling, express them in healthy ways such as confiding in a friend, journaling, or seeking solace in prayer. This acknowledgment honors your experience, paving the way for the next phase.

❖ **Decide to Forgive:** Forgiveness is a conscious choice, not solely guided by emotions. Even if you don't feel ready to forgive, you can make the decision to do so. This act of the will empowers you to take control of your life and happiness, opening the door to healing and peace.

❖ **Understand the Other Person:** Forgiveness doesn't imply agreement or justification of the actions that caused pain. Instead, seek to understand the other person's perspective and motives. Questions like why they acted as they did, their emotions at the time, and their needs or fears humanize and empathize, acknowledging their flaws and brokenness.

❖ **Release the Other Person:** Forgiveness doesn't mandate reconciliation or trust with the person who caused hurt but entails releasing them from judgment and resentment. Affirm to yourself or them: "I forgive you for what you did. I release you from my anger and bitterness. I wish you well, and I hope you find peace." This release liberates you from the burden of carrying pain and grudges, allowing you to move forward.

❖ **Forgive Yourself:** Extend the act of forgiveness not only to others but also to yourself. Forgive any mistakes, regrets, or self-blame. Accept and love yourself, saying: "I forgive myself for what I did or didn't do. I accept myself for who I am. I love myself, and I am worthy of love." This self-forgiveness heals self-esteem, restores self-confidence, and rebuilds your relationship with yourself and with God.

❖ **Seek God's Forgiveness:** Acknowledge that forgiveness is not solely a human act but also a divine gift. God, the source of all forgiveness, is always ready to extend His mercy, no matter our past actions. Repent, confess, and seek His forgiveness, experiencing His grace and joy. Through this, you recognize your need for Him and His transformative power.

Forgiveness is undoubtedly challenging, but it is within reach. Far from a sign of weakness, forgiveness is a testament to strength. It's not a burden but a blessing, paving the road to healing, happiness, and holiness. Forgiveness is the journey to God, who is close to the brokenhearted and heals their wounds (Psalm 147:3).

# CHAPTER 8

## *The Art Of Self-Discovery: Transforming Heartbreak Into Personal Growth*

Heartbreak, despite its painful nature, possesses the potential to act as a powerful catalyst for personal growth and self-discovery. Within the realm of shattered emotions and the feeling of loss, an opportunity arises to embark on a profound journey of self-understanding and embrace transformative changes.

✓ **Embracing Change:** Heartbreak often propels individuals into a period of upheaval and transformation. In this chapter, we delve into strategies for navigating this transformative process with intention and purpose. Here are key steps to master the art of self-discovery amid the challenges of heartbreak:

✓ **Reflect on the Experience:** Take dedicated time to contemplate the heartbreak and its impact on your life. What lessons can be extracted from this experience? What patterns or behaviors have emerged? Reflecting on the pain offers valuable insights into your vulnerabilities, strengths, and areas for growth.

✓ **Explore Your Emotions:** Heartbreak elicits a range of emotions—sadness, anger, confusion. Rather than suppressing these feelings, approach them with curiosity. Understanding this spectrum of emotions allows for a more profound connection with oneself. Journaling, confiding in a trusted friend, or seeking professional support can facilitate this exploration.

✓ **Rediscover Your Passions:** Often, personal passions and interests take a backseat amid relationships. Utilize this time to rediscover what genuinely brings you joy. Whether it's reviving a forgotten hobby, embracing a creative pursuit, or acquiring a new skill, reconnecting with your passions fosters a sense of purpose and fulfillment.

✓ **Set Personal Goals:** Establishing new goals, whether substantial or minor, provides a roadmap for personal growth. These goals may relate to your career, self-improvement, or pursuing experiences you've always desired. Accomplishing these goals instills a sense of achievement and empowers you to shape your narrative.

✓ **Cultivate Self-Compassion:** Be gentle with yourself during this tumultuous period. Self-compassion entails treating yourself with the same kindness and understanding you would extend to a friend facing challenges. Embracing self-compassion paves the way for healing and self-discovery.

✓ **Challenge Limiting Beliefs:** Heartbreak may inadvertently reinforce negative self-perceptions. Identify and challenge these limiting beliefs. Acknowledge your strengths, resilience, and capacity for growth. Overcoming heartbreak becomes an opportunity to rewrite your narrative and foster a more positive self-image.

✓ **A Strong Support System:** Surround yourself with a supportive network of friends, family, or even a therapist who can aid in the process of self-discovery. Sharing your journey with others not only provides emotional support but also offers diverse perspectives on personal growth.

The art of self-discovery unfolds as a process that leverages heartbreak as an opportunity for growth. It involves transforming pain into power, loss into gain, and tragedy into triumph. It is the journey of uncovering the silver lining, discovering hidden treasures, and witnessing the rainbow after the storm. Ultimately, it is the process of evolving into the best version of ourselves—the version that God created us to be.

# CHAPTER 9

## *The Power Of Gratitude: How To Cultivate Gratitude And Find Joy In The Present Moment*

Gratitude stands out as one of the most potent and positive emotions available to us. It transcends mere feelings; it is a habit, a practice, and a lifestyle that, when embraced daily, transforms our outlook on life. Gratitude involves acknowledging the goodness and grace surrounding us each day, expressing love and joy for the gifts bestowed upon us by both God and others.

This chapter delves into the profound impact of gratitude, not only on our emotional and mental well-being but also on our physical and spiritual health. Research has shown that gratitude increases happiness, reduces stress, enhances resilience, improves relationships, and even boosts the immune system. It is a powerful force that draws us closer to God, aligning us with His presence and providence, as emphasized in 1 Thessalonians 5:18: "Give thanks in all circumstances; for this is God's will for you in Christ Jesus."

## Cultivating Gratitude: A Daily Practice

Commence Your Day with Gratitude: Initiate each day by expressing gratitude. Thank God for the gift of another day, an opportunity to live, love, and serve. Acknowledge specific blessings such as health, family, friends, work, or talents. Set a positive tone and nurture a grateful attitude for the day ahead.

❖ **Maintain a Gratitude Journal:** Chronicle your blessings by keeping a gratitude journal. List at least three things you're grateful for each day, irrespective of how small. Reflect on why you're thankful for them and the emotions they evoke. Whether it's a compliment, a smile, a hug, or the beauty of nature, document moments of joy to build a treasury of memories.

❖ **Extend Gratitude to Others:** Actively show appreciation and thankfulness to those who have supported, inspired, or challenged you. Whether through a card, a note, a call, or a text, convey your gratitude. Strengthen relationships, spread love, and share joy by expressing your thanks to others.

❖ **Practice Gratitude Meditation:** Engage in gratitude meditation to deepen your awareness and consciousness. Meditate on the things you're grateful for, the emotions they evoke, and the source of your gratitude. This practice enhances inner peace and harmony, connecting you with God and others on a profound level.

❖ **Live in the Present Moment:** Embrace the power of gratitude by living in the present moment. Focus on the here and now, savoring each experience without dwelling on the past or worrying about the future. Appreciate what you have, relish the moment, and declare, "This is the opportunity, the gift."

## The Power of Gratitude: A Lifestyle

Gratitude is not an occasional occurrence but a consistent, intentional practice and a way of life. It shapes our perspective, steering us away from taking things for granted and encouraging us to celebrate and share our gratitude with the world.

In essence, gratitude is the power of joy, and joy is the power of God. As we actively cultivate gratitude in our daily lives, we tap into a transformative force that not only enriches our well-being but also radiates positivity to those around us. Gratitude is the key to unlocking the profound joy inherent in the present moment, connecting us with God and infusing our lives with purpose and meaning.

# CHAPTER 10

## *Journey To Heal: The Hope Of a New Beginning And a Brighter Future*

Healing from heartbreak is not a destination, but a journey. It is not a point in time, but a process. It is not a linear path, but a winding road. It is not a smooth ride, but a bumpy one. It is not a solo trip, but a shared one.

Healing from heartbreak is a journey that involves ups and downs, twists and turns, stops and starts, detours and shortcuts, setbacks and breakthroughs. It is a journey that requires courage, patience, perseverance, and faith. It is a journey that offers challenges, lessons, insights, and growth. It is a journey that leads to healing, happiness, and holiness.

Healing from heartbreak is a journey that has a beginning, but no end. It is a journey that starts with a broken heart but ends with a whole heart. It is a journey that starts with a wound but ends with a scar. It is a journey that starts with a loss but ends with a gain. It is a journey that starts with a tragedy but ends with a triumph.

Healing from heartbreak is a journey that has hope, but no guarantee. It is a journey that has a direction, but no destination. It is a journey that has a purpose, but no plan. It is a journey that has a vision, but no sight. It is a journey that has a promise, but no proof.

Healing from heartbreak is a journey that is guided by God, but influenced by us. It is a journey that is initiated by God, but completed by us. It is a journey that is supported by God but challenged by us. It is a journey that is blessed by God, but shared by us. It is a journey that is designed by God but lived by us.

How can we embark on the journey to heal? How can we cope with the pain and the grief that we feel? How can we embrace the hope and the joy that we seek? **Here are some steps that can help you on your journey:**

- **Trust in God:** The first step to healing is to trust in God. You need to believe that God is with you, that He loves you, and that He has a plan for you. You need to surrender your heart, your will, and your life to Him. You need to rely on His strength, His grace, and His wisdom. You need to say to Him or yourself: "I trust in You. I love You. I follow You." By trusting in God, you are acknowledging your dependence on Him and your confidence in Him.

- **Seek help:** The second step to healing is to seek help. You need to reach out to the people who care about you, who understand you, and who can support you. You need to seek professional help, such as a counselor, a therapist, or a coach, who can guide you, advise you, and empower you. You need to seek spiritual help, such as a pastor, a mentor, or a friend, who can pray for you, encourage you, and inspire you. You need to say to them or yourself: "I need help. I accept help. I appreciate the help." By seeking help, you are recognizing your need for others and your openness to others.

- **Heal yourself:** The third step to healing is to heal yourself. You need to take care of your physical, emotional, mental, and spiritual health. You need to eat well, sleep well, exercise well, and rest well. You need to express your feelings, process your thoughts, release your stress, and nurture your joy. You need to meditate, pray, read, and learn. You need to say to yourself or your body, your mind, your heart, or your soul: "I heal myself. I love myself. I respect myself." By healing yourself, you are honoring your dignity and your worth.

- **Forgive:** The fourth step to healing is to forgive. You need to forgive the person who hurt you, the situation that caused you pain, and yourself for your mistakes. You need to let go of the resentment, the bitterness, and the anger that are holding you back from healing and happiness. You need to say to them or yourself: "I forgive you. I release you. I wish you well." By forgiving, you are freeing yourself from the past and opening yourself to the future.

- **Move on:** The fifth step to healing is to move on. You need to accept the reality of what happened, the finality of what ended, and the possibility of what can happen. You need to embrace the change, the challenge, and the opportunity that lies ahead. You need to say to yourself or the world: "I move on. I grow on. I live on." By moving on, you are creating your present and your potential.

Healing from heartbreak is not a destination, but a journey. It is not a point in time, but a process. It is not a linear path, but a winding road. It is not a smooth ride, but a bumpy one. It is not a solo trip, but a shared one.

Healing from heartbreak is a journey that involves ups and downs, twists and turns, stops and starts, detours and shortcuts, setbacks and breakthroughs. It is a journey that requires courage, patience, perseverance, and faith. It is a journey that offers challenges, lessons, insights, and growth. It is a journey that leads to healing, happiness, and holiness.

Healing from heartbreak is a journey that has a beginning, but no end. It is a journey that starts with a broken heart but ends with a whole heart. It is a journey that starts with a wound but ends with a scar. It is a journey that starts with a loss but ends with a gain. It is a journey that starts with a tragedy but ends with a triumph.

Healing from heartbreak is a journey that has hope, but no guarantee. It is a journey that has a direction, but no destination. It is a journey that has a purpose, but no plan. It is a journey that has a vision, but no sight. It is a journey that has a promise, but no proof.

Healing from heartbreak is a journey that is guided by God, but influenced by us. It is a journey that is initiated by God, but completed by us. It is a journey that is supported by God but challenged by us. It is a journey that is blessed by God, but shared by us. It is a journey that is designed by God but lived by us.

Healing from heartbreak is the journey to heal. Healing from heartbreak is the journey to hope. Healing from heartbreak is the journey to God.

# CONCLUSION

## *How To Live With a Grateful And Joyful Heart*

Have you ever felt so alone and hurt that you cried out to God for help? Sometimes we think that we are the only ones who suffer, but that is not true. God allows us to go through trials so that we can share our testimonies with others. Our testimonies are the tools that God uses to help others overcome their challenges and reveal His glory. Revelation 12:11 KJV says, "And they overcame him by the blood of the Lamb, and by the word of their testimony". This means that we should tell others what God has done for us, no matter how bad things seem. God is faithful and He will keep His promises. This is how we overcome.

I know how it feels to be brokenhearted. This world has taken so much from me, and maybe you have lost something too. When we hit rock bottom, the world cannot help us. That is why we often turn to Jesus Christ when we have nothing left. We need a Savior, and we run to the One who can save us and our souls.

As I wrote this book, God healed my broken heart. When I started this journey, I did not know how I would pay for a place to live or what I should do next in my life, my purpose, my destiny, and my obedience to God. My family and I are living in a hotel with no savings. I work, but most of my paycheck goes to the hotel room. I am telling you this because I want you to know that I am with you. I am also brokenhearted and confused about what God is doing in my life.

But you know what? I am starting to see God's plan. He has brought my family and me through so much in the past few years, and now I can see how He is working everything for our good. God has not forgotten us. Please remember that. He has not forgotten us. He will never leave us or forsake us. He has plans for us, plans to prosper us and to give us hope and a future. It may not look like anything is happening, but trust God. He is in control. He is doing so much for you behind the scenes, especially if you have faith and believe in Him.

If you are struggling, let us pray that God will increase your faith.

*Dear Heavenly Father, we bless and praise Your name. Father, we ask You to forgive our sins. We thank You for Your mercy and grace. You are everything to us. Father, we need You more than ever. You know our situation right now. We thank You for giving us strength and we ask that You keep being our strength when we are weak. Father, our faith is low. Please increase our faith, so that we will not doubt You when we know what You can do in an instant. Forgive us, Father, for any complaints or anything in our hearts that is not like You. Help us to be more like You and less like ourselves. We thank and praise Your name. In Jesus' name, we pray, Amen.*

Our prayers do not have to be long or fancy to reach God's ears. The most important thing is to always thank Him, always ask for forgiveness (repent), and always acknowledge who God is to us (our Heavenly Father or our Father).

I experienced my first heartbreak as a teenager and I looked for books or anything that could help me cope or understand. I know that God is a healer and that He gives us wisdom, but I wanted to see evidence from others who had gone through the same thing. I wanted to see that things would change and get better, but I did not find what I was looking for. God took me through this because He wanted me to write this book to help others who need God and also need guidance on how to overcome their situation.

As I keep learning and unlearning things, I am amazed at how we humans tend to run to everything except God. I am guilty of this myself. I would sometimes sleep to try to escape from what I was going through. I used to say that I had suffered enough and that I could not take it anymore. God showed me that I could do more than I thought. He showed me what He could do through me. Guys, I am writing this book to help others, and I am homeless.

My family and I becoming homeless was simple we trusted a family member who promised to help us after we obeyed God and moved across the country. We learned that we have to be careful who we let into our circle when we follow God's will. God gave us the vision, not everyone else. If we are married, God gave us the vision and our spouse supports us or He gave both of us the vision. Other people are not part of what God is doing for us or in us. So when our situation was not aligned with God's plan, He moved us out of that place and that family member's house. He also revealed to us the true motive behind their so-called help. Not everyone is for us and our journey. Some people just want to sabotage from within.

God had a plan for us that we did not understand. When we became homeless, I thought that God had abandoned us. I felt like I could not hear from God. I felt like I had made a mistake. I did not understand how God could let us be in a place where we had no one, no place to go, and no place to sleep. I felt like God was not real. He would never do something like this to my family. My husband did not deserve this. He had suffered enough. My daughters did not choose this life. I brought them into this world. Why would He do this to them? Why were we going through this? Why were we going through so much? What did we do in life to deserve this? I was depressed, embarrassed, helpless, and felt stupid. I felt God was no longer with us, and I felt like I was now hurting my family. All the things I worried about weren't important.

God quickly showed me that He was with us, but I still felt depressed and embarrassed. He showed me that only He could help me with this situation. I just needed to trust God. I needed to let go of control and trust God. When I prayed with my family and let go of control, things started to change for us. We were still homeless, but we had faith that God could change our situation in a moment. We had faith that God was in control. We had faith that God would never leave us or forsake us. We had faith that things were working out for us. I had faith that God chose me and my family to do His will on earth, to show others that no matter how things look right now, things will and can get better. Things will be better sooner than we think, we just have to have faith in God.

You have reached the end of this book, but not the end of your journey to heal. In fact, this is just the beginning of a new chapter in your life, one that is filled with hope, grace, and joy. My goal in writing this book was to help you overcome heartbreak and find hope in God's presence and promises. I wanted to share with you the lessons and strategies that have helped me and many others to heal from the wounds of the past and embrace the future with confidence and optimism.

**In this book, you have learned:**

1.    What it means to be brokenhearted, and how God is close to you and saves you in your distress. (Chapter 1)

2.    The importance of faith, and how faith can help you to trust God, overcome fear, and face challenges with courage. (Chapter 2)

3.   The role of prayer, and how prayer can help you to communicate with God, receive His guidance, and experience His peace. (Chapter 3)

4.   The nature of God, and how God heals your wounds, restores your joy, and transforms your life. (Chapter 4)

5.   The stages of grief, and how to cope with the different emotions and reactions that you may experience after a loss or a breakup. (Chapter 5)

6.   The strength of community, and how to find and build a supportive network of people who can help you to heal, grow, and thrive. (Chapter 6)

7.   The journey to forgiveness, and how to forgive yourself and others, and release the pain, anger, and resentment that may hold you back. (Chapter 7)

8.   The art of self-discovery, and how to use heartbreak as an opportunity to learn more about yourself, your values, your strengths, and your passions. (Chapter 8)

9.   The power of gratitude, and how to cultivate gratitude and find joy in the present moment, regardless of your circumstances. (Chapter 9)

10.  The journey to heal, and how to move forward with hope, faith, and love, and embrace the new

opportunities and possibilities that await you. (Chapter 10)

Living with a grateful and joyful heart is not only possible but also desirable and beneficial for you and those around you. When you live with a grateful and joyful heart, you:

- Experience more peace, happiness, and satisfaction in your life.

- Become more resilient, adaptable, and optimistic in the face of difficulties.

- Heal faster and more completely from the wounds of the past.

- Grow stronger and wiser from the lessons of the present.

- Fulfill your potential and purpose in the future.

As a famous author and speaker once said, "Gratitude is the healthiest of all human emotions. The more you express gratitude for what you have, the more likely you will have even more to express gratitude for."

But living with a grateful and joyful heart is not something that happens automatically or overnight. It is something that you have to choose and practice every day until it becomes a habit and a lifestyle. It is something that you have to cultivate and nurture, like a garden or a plant.

How can you do that? **Here are some practical tips, suggestions, and resources to help you get started:**

**\*Keep a gratitude journal:** where you write down at least three things that you are grateful for every day. You can use a notebook, a phone app, or a website to do this. You can also share your gratitude with others, such as your family, friends, or social media followers.

**\*Pray daily:** and thank God for His presence, His promises, and His blessings in your life. You can also ask Him for His help, His guidance, and His wisdom in any situation that you may face. You can use your own words, or follow a prayer book, a devotional, or a podcast to guide you.

**\*Read the Bible daily:** and meditate on God's words, His character, and His works. You can use a Bible app, a website, or a book to help you read and understand the Scriptures. You can also join a Bible study group, a church, or an online community to learn and grow with others.

**\*Listen to uplifting music, podcasts, or audiobooks that inspire you, motivate you, and fill you with joy.**

**\*Watch inspiring videos, movies, or shows that entertain you, educate you, and make you smile.**

**\*Read inspiring books, articles, or blogs that inform you, challenge you, and spark your curiosity.**

**\*Do something creative:** Such as writing, drawing, painting, singing, dancing, or cooking. You can use your own talents, skills, and interests, or learn something new. You can also share your creations with others, or enjoy them yourself.

**\*Do something fun:** Such as playing a game, doing a puzzle, going for a walk, or visiting a park. You can do something that you enjoy, or try something different. You can also invite others to join you or have some alone time.

**\*Do something kind:** such as helping a neighbor, volunteering for a cause, donating to a charity, or sending a card. You can do something that you care about, or discover a new way to make a difference. You can also receive kindness from others or appreciate the kindness around you.

These are just some of the ways that you can live with a grateful and joyful heart. You can find more ideas, tips, and resources online.

I hope that this book has been helpful and encouraging for you and that you have found some value and inspiration in it. I would love to hear from you and know how you are doing on your journey to heal. You can contact me through my website, my email, or my social media accounts, which are listed at the end of this book. You can also leave a review, a comment, or a question on the platform where you purchased or accessed this book. I appreciate your feedback, your questions, and your testimonies.

Thank you for reading this book, and for allowing me to share my story and wisdom with you. I am grateful for you and for the opportunity to serve you. I pray that God will bless you, heal you, and fill you with His joy and peace. I wish you all the best on your journey to healing, and I look forward to hearing from you soon.

**May the Lord bless you and keep you;**

**May the Lord make his face shine on you and be gracious to you;**

**May the Lord turn his face toward you and give you peace. (Numbers 6:24-26)**

# SCRIPTURES AND PRAYERS

## *God Is Close To The Brokenhearted*

*Almighty God, we come to you in complete surrender. In our fragility, we find solace in your love.*

*We thank you that you are near to the brokenhearted. You do not turn away from us in our moments of strife or despair, but instead come and walk beside us.*

*We offer our struggles and sadness to You, believing that You will give us strength and courage when we are weak. Help us to remember that we can always count on Your presence, even in our darkest hours.*

*But most of all, let us remember that You always hear our prayers. Thank you for your grace, faithfulness, and understanding. Thank you for loving us so deeply, and for never forsaking us, even when we feel as if we are alone.*

*We praise and honor You, and give You our deepest love.*
*Amen.*

### Psalm 34:18

*O Lord, we come before You today in humble prayer. We thank You for the many blessings and provisions You have made for us. We give You thanks for the promise contained in Psalm 34:18: "The Lord is close to the brokenhearted and saves those who are crushed in spirit."*

*Lord, we know that You know our need for comfort and strength during trying times. We come to You in our distress and ask that You wrap us in Your loving arms. Give us the courage to endure our struggles, and the wisdom to understand Your will in our lives.*

*Provide us with the peace and comfort that only You can offer. Help us to find trust and faith in You, even in the midst of turmoil and danger. Increase our love for one another, and remind us that our connection with You will help us build a stronger bond that will last for eternity.*

*We thank You for never leaving our side, even when life gets difficult. We place all our worries, doubts, and fears in*

*Your loving hands. In the power of Your name, we thank You and pray. Amen.*

### Jeremiah 29:11

*Heavenly Father,*

*We humbly pray that you bless us, and every one of us, with the hope and peace that comes from Jeremiah 29:11.*

*We lift up our praises and thank you for leading us with your promises of "plans to prosper us and not to harm us, plans to give us hope and a future."*

*Help us to remember that when our future looks uncertain, you are there, guiding our way, and opening us to all the good plans and outcomes that you are creating for us.*

*We trust that you are directing us towards a future that lies in your hands.*

*We pray that you will fill us with the courage to keep following you, no matter what may be before us. We know that your plans for us will be for our benefit, and will give us a wonderful future.*

*Amen.*

## Heartbreak

*Father God,*

*We come before you in prayer, seeking strength and peace for all those who are struggling with heartbreak. Lord, we know this can be a difficult time, of sadness and pain. Yet we know in you, and through your love, light, and mercy, that you can bring solace to our hearts and souls.*

*We ask that you wrap your loving arms around us all each and every day. Give us strength to get through our difficult times, and to be an anchor and light as we try to make sense of our emotions. And help us to find the beauty in our mistakes, as you always offer us a chance to learn, grow, and be transformed.*

*We thank you for your unconditional and infinite love, your mercy, and your graciousness. Help us to turn to you in times of trouble, and find hope and forgiveness when heartbreak washes over us. In Jesus 'Name, we pray, Amen.*

## Homelessness

God,

*We come to You asking for Your presence and help in the face of the homelessness crisis.*

*We pray for those affected by it, that their emotional, physical, and spiritual needs be met.*

*We ask that those in power and positions of influence respond to this ongoing crisis with wisdom and compassion.*

*Equip them with the resources to effectively address the root causes and symptoms of homelessness.*

*We pray that the necessary support and assistance is given to those in need.*

*Bring resources to the communities and individuals who are striving to do something to address this issue and see it diminished.*

*Give us the courage to confront and challenge injustice and indifference, so that we may fulfill our vital role as co-creators in the renewal of our world.*

*God, hear our prayer and grant us your blessing.*

*Amen.*

### Homeless

*Heavenly Father,*

*We come before you today to ask for your help and guidance for those affected by homelessness. We pray for the safety, protection, and provision for those who are without a home, and we pray for an end to this troubling situation.*

*We ask you to provide them with shelter, food, and warmth in these difficult times. Give them strength to find hope in their current situation and help them find a true path forward. Give them the courage to face the road ahead and fill them with faith to persevere in the face of adversity.*

*We pray for the organizations and individuals dedicated to providing aid to those affected by homelessness. Help them to continue their work and to help these individuals find stability in their lives.*

*In your name, we pray, Amen.*

## Home

*Loving God,*

*We come to You, praying for all those who need a safe and secure place to call home. Provide for all those who are homeless, hapless, and desperate for shelter. Be their refuge and their strength.*

*Grant them access to the places that will offer them comfort and safety. Help them find the resources they need to find a space that will fit their needs.*

*Guide those willing to lend help to extend their arms and fill the needs of those who lack a place to lay their head at night. Strengthen those providing assistance and fill their hearts with loving compassion as they make a difference.*

*We thank You for Your hope, for Your promise of goodness and Providence. Let all who need a home find shelter, love, and support. Amen.*

## Penniless/No money

*Heavenly Father, we come humbly before you to ask that you would provide for those in need. For those who are struggling due to a lack of money, we pray that you will surround them with your protection and provision.*

*May those who are in a state of poverty be filled with hope and strength knowing that you are their faithful provider. Soften the hearts of those who are able to give and provide, so that they would be generous and compassionate towards those in poverty.*

*We thank you for the abundant blessings that you have given us so that we can share with those in need. Redeem and restore those lives that are chained by a lack of financial resources. Help us to see people in need as more than just "less fortunate" but as divinely loved and special individuals as they are.*

*In Jesus 'name, amen.*

### Financially stable

*Lord, we come before you in prayer, humbly asking for financial stability. We acknowledge that all things come from you and you are our loving provider.*

*Help us to have a proper attitude toward money, never greed or covetousness, but a desire to share with others and use our resources to do Your work. Instill in us the ability to manage our money responsibly.*

*Give us the energy to follow through with wise decisions concerning our finances. Lead us toward good financial investments that hold long-term benefits.*

*Anoint us with creativity and new ideas to increase our resources while maintaining our indebtment.*

*Bless the work of our hands, so that we may have more to give to those in need.*

*Thank you, Lord, for securing finances now and in the future. We thank you that you are our help in times of trouble and you will never leave or forsake us.*

*In Jesus 'Name, Amen.*


### In debt

*Heavenly Father,*

*We come to you humbly, asking for your help during this difficult time. We have become in debt and feel overwhelmed by it. Please bring us the courage and strength to keep going and help us to make the needed changes to get us out of debt.*

*We ask that you give us patience, endurance, and guidance to make smart decisions as we take the steps to pay off our debt. Grant us wisdom to know when to save and when to spend, so that we can free ourselves from the burden of debt.*

*Give us hope that tomorrow will be better than today and that one day we will have the financial freedom to make the choices we need to live joyful, debt-free lives. We know you can turn our despair into joy, and that you will not forsake us at this time.*

*We give you thanks and praise in Jesus' name. Amen.*


### *100% debt free*

*Dear Heavenly Father,*

*We come before you in prayer, asking for your divine help in eliminating debt in our lives. We recognize that we have financially overextended ourselves and now feel overwhelmed by the debt that looms over us. Please forgive us for our irresponsible choices and grant us patience, discipline, and knowledge to learn from our mistakes.*

*Enable us to take a view of our finances, revealing opportunities for savings, investments, and financial prosperity. Provide us with sound financial advice and help us to make decisions that will lead to positive outcomes.*

*Instill in us the commitment and determination it will take to make the necessary sacrifices and choices for us to become debt-free. Encourage us when times get tough and grant us the strength and resolve we need to stay focused on our goal of becoming debt-free.*

*Most of all, Lord, help us to be humble and mindful of our financial situation. Teach us to live within our means and seek guidance from you throughout this process.*

*We thank you in advance for your divine intervention and ask that you grant us the blessing of debt freedom.*

*Amen.*

### Isaiah 41:10 AMP

*Almighty God,*

*We gather in prayer, giving you glory, giving you thanks for your faithfulness and power, shown in Isaiah 41:10. You are always there for us, reassuring us to not fear, to not be dismayed, for we will not be forgotten.*

*Your Word speaks to us, your people, so that we may be reminded to be strong and courageous and not be dismayed even when facing the most difficult of life's struggles. Your faithfulness gives us courage and strength to press on and not give in to fear or doubt.*

*We pray that your Spirit will guide us, and give us wisdom and discernment so that our thoughts and actions will reflect you. Your love cares for us, comforts us, and strengthens us. Thank you for your promises, your mighty acts, and the glorious hope that you have given us to cling to. Amen.*

## Psalms 147:3 AMP

*Heavenly Father, we praise Your glorious name in recognition of all Your blessings. You have so much knowledge that the number of Your thoughts is countless and Your wisdom is greater than our minds could comprehend. We know that You heal the brokenhearted and bind up their wounds. We come to You today with grateful hearts, thanking You for Your goodness and provision.*

*Lord, we ask that You would open our ears and our understanding to hear Your Word of truth. We desire to marvel at Your mighty deeds and recognize Your sovereignty over all things. As Your Word says in Psalm 147:3, "He heals the brokenhearted and binds up their wounds."*

*Help us to show compassion and care to those who are struggling, while always keeping in mind that with You, nothing is too hard. Provide an ever-flowing fountain of love and grace over those who are dealing with brokenness. Lord, help us to strengthen the weak and comfort the afflicted and believe in Your power to ease any suffering.*

*We praise You for Your infinite goodness and Your unfailing love. You are our Rock, our Fortress, and our Strength. In Jesus' Name, Amen.*

### James 5:14 AMP

*Heavenly Father, we come to You in thanksgiving for the words of James 5:13 AMP. This scripture reminds us to pray earnestly at all times and in all places. Lord, we pray for Your guidance, wisdom, and strength and those who are suffering. Give them Your peace, and comfort, and rest in knowing that they can come to You in prayer and have faith that You will answer. Grant friends, family, and allies, courage, hope, and understanding during seasons of suffering. Provide everyone with the opportunity to draw near to You in faith, to serve, and to trust You in all matters. As they surrender to Your will, may Your light shine*

*through them and reflect hope and resilience everywhere.*
*Amen.*

### *Isaiah 61:1 AMP*

*Gracious and loving God, we come to you in the spirit of Isaiah 61:1. We humbly ask that the spirit of the Lord be upon us and that the spirit of wisdom and understanding be our guide in every aspect of our lives.*

*Help us to bear our burdens with love, patience, and kindness, and that You fill our spirits with joy in our moments of despair. May You grant us victory over the oppressors who challenge our faith, love, and freedom.*

*May Your spirit touch the hearts of those who are broken, leading them away from despair and fear, but towards Your loving arms. All around us, there is darkness, but by Your grace, that darkness can and will be turned into light.*

*We thank You for Your constant presence in our lives, and the love You have shown us. We offer our love, respect, and praise to You this day. May our spirits be uplifted and strengthened through Your mercy and grace. Amen.*

### Psalm 46:1-2 AMP

*Almighty God, we give thanks for the promise of Your strength and guidance in times of distress and confusion. You provide a place of safety and peace for us, even in the midst of chaos.*

*We ask that You would be with us, Lord, as we go through hard times. We know that You are always there for us. We place our trust in You, and we rely on Your loving arms to keep us safe.*

*We also ask that You help us to be brave and strong when life's storms come our way. Help us to remember the promise of Psalm 46:1-2 (AMP), that You are our refuge and strength, a very present help in trouble.*

*Let us trust in You and find the courage to endure the hard times. Help us to not forget who You are and all the good You have done for us and the world. Lord, comfort us in our darkest moments and open us up to Your truth and guidance. In Your loving name, Amen.*

**Psalm 55:22 AMP**

*Almighty and everlasting God, we come to You in prayer. We bow before You and seek Your protection and grace. We thank You for the gift of love that comes through Your Word and comes from Your teachings.*

*We pray that according to Psalm 55:22, You would cast all our anxieties on You, for You care for us. When we feel overwhelmed, help us to pause and remember that You alone offer us Your support and strength. Give us the courage and faith to trust in Your provision throughout all the tough times in our lives.*

*Protect us from all anxious thoughts and let us feel Your peace within our hearts. Draw us gently back to You, that we may be restored and our spirits renewed in You. May we find comfort, joy, hope, and strength in Your presence.*

*Use our faith to guide us ever closer to You. Amen.*

**Psalm 62:8 AMP**

*O Heavenly Father,*

*We thank You for your Word and the beauty of your love that You generously extend to us all.*

*We humbly seek Your care and protection, especially today. As we read in Psalm 62:8, "Trust in, lean on, rely on, and have confidence in Him at all times, you people; pour out your hearts before Him. God is our refuge (our Rock, our Fortress, and our High Tower)."*

*We pray that You would fill us with an assurance of Your faithfulness over our lives. Please help us to trust in You, lean on You, and lay our burdens at Your feet.*

*We pray that all our fears and worries would become your burdens, O God and that our faith in Your goodness and mercy would become strong. Thank You for being our Refuge, our Fortress, and Stronghold. We shout You are the Sovereign King of kings.*

*In Jesus' precious name, Amen.*


### Psalm 71:20 AMP

*Almighty God, we come to you in praise and thank you for your unfailing love. We give you glory and honor for the fact that you are our protection and confidant, and we seek refuge in your shadow from the schemes of the enemy.*

*We pray for your strength and guidance in all that we do as we express our hope and assurance in this life that you will deliver us. Your word is our source of strength, and we pray for faith to trust and believe your promises in Psalm 71:20.*

*Help us to never abandon the hope and security that comes through your Word and never give up on the goodness of your deeds or the joy of your salvation. Teach us to hold fast to You and never to forget the work that You have done in our lives.*

*We ask for courage and blessings as we live each day. Through your mercy, we pray that You would bring us closer to You and uplift us, as our joy and delight. We worship and adore You and give You all glory and honor, now and forever. Amen.*

### Lamentations 3:22 AMP

*Oh Lord, we come to You with humility to acknowledge You as the source of all hope and mercy. Thank You for the peace and security You provide and for Your faithful and all-encompassing love.*

*Help us to understand Your deep compassion when it feels like darkness surrounds us and we cry out to You. Remind us of Your promise in Lamentations 3:22 AMP, "The Lord's loving-kindnesses indeed never cease, for His compassions never fail."*

*We praise You for hearing our pleas and meeting our needs. Give us Your strength and grace each day to persevere and remain hopeful in this life.*

*Grant us the resolve to remain faithful, to trust in You, and to keep Your commands. In Jesus 'precious name, we pray, Amen.*

### John 16:33 AMP

*Father God,*

*We come to You with a full heart of faith and humble obedience. We know that You are with us in our struggles, our joys, and our tears.*

*Help us to remember Your Word that states, "I[Jesus] have told you these things, so that in me you may have peace. In this world you will have trouble. But take heart! I have overcome the world." (John 16:33 AMP).*

*We lift up our Savior, Jesus Christ, and ask You to help us remember that He has overcome our obstacles and will grant us peace as we continue to walk in faith. Let us rest in knowing that no matter what trials may come our way,*

*You are with us in the struggle and You are the victor who brings us success.*

*We ask You to grant peace to all who require it and join us in declaring that Jesus has overcome the world.*

*Thank You, Heavenly Father, for Your protection and wisdom. In Jesus' name, Amen.*


### *2 Corinthians 4:8-10 NLT*

*Loving and Powerful God,*

*We thank you for your unfailing love and mercy. We are comforted to know that, even during our struggles, we can rely on you. Help us to remember that we do not have to carry all the burdens of life on our own. Guide us through the darkness and renew our strength. Grant us hope for our future with the knowledge that you will never leave our side.*

*We ask for your continual presence as we take on the challenges life presents us so that we might have the courage to face our fears. Protect us from feeling overwhelmed by the pain and suffering of this world and show us how to focus our eyes on the hope you have promised us.*

*Remind us to find joy and peace in knowing that all earthly troubles will one day pass and that eternal love awaits us. Today, we seek fortitude in the words of 2 Corinthians 4: 8-10: "We are pressed on every side by troubles, but we are not crushed. We are perplexed, but not driven to despair. We are hunted down but never abandoned by God. We get knocked down, but we are not destroyed."*

*You are our Refuge, Amen.*


### 1 Peter 5:7 AMP

*Dear Lord,*

*We humbly come before you, thankful for the hope and peace we have in You. We pray to You for help in our struggles and anxieties of life, trusting that You are our ever-present help in trouble.*

*Lord, we commit to You our cares, surrendering them humbly into Your loving care. Help us to remain at peace and not worry by understanding that You care for us as our Father.*

*We pray over the words of 1 Peter 5:7 in the Amplified Bible, which states, "casting all your cares upon Him, for He cares for us." Help us to know that nothing is too small to bring to You. Help us to call on You and trust that when we do, You are already bringing the right answers and solutions into our lives.*

*As children of Yours, You are deeply committed to us and constantly caring for us. Thank You, Lord, for Your goodness and faithfulness.*

*We pray this in the matchless name of Jesus, Amen.*

### Revelation 21:4 KJV

*Heavenly Father, thank you for your promises found in Revelation 21:4. We are amazed and humbled by your love. We thank you for comforting us and helping us to understand that our lives are in your hands.*

*Fill our hearts and minds with peace, thankfulness, and assurance in this time of anticipation and uncertainty. Grant us a renewed hope that your plan for this world and its inhabitants will bring us to experience complete joy and satisfaction.*

*We pray that you will continue to lead us in paths of righteousness so that we might live in faith and obedience to your will. As we pass through times of trials, grant us the strength and courage to face any situation with confidence that comes from our faith in you.*

*Above all, we thank you for your complete love that is beyond any of our understanding, in Jesus 'Name, Amen.*

# CONTACT INFORMATION

**WEBSITE:** www.wearethemartins.com

**EMAIL:** antonioandmelanie@wearethemartins.com

**FACEBOOK:** Melanie Martin
https://www.facebook.com/melanie.mays.56

**INSTAGRAM:** mrsmelaniemartin
https://www.instagram.com/mrsmelaniemartin

**YouTube:** We Are The Martins
https://youtube.com/@wearethemartins

**PO Box:** PO BOX 181063 Utica, MI 48318.

Made in United States
Orlando, FL
15 June 2024

47923445R10052